American Symbols
AND THEIR Meanings

THE
DECLARATION
OF
INDEPENDENCE

American Symbols
AND THEIR Meanings

THE ALAMO
THE AMERICAN FLAG
THE BALD EAGLE
THE CONFEDERATE FLAG
THE CONSTITUTION
THE DECLARATION OF INDEPENDENCE
ELLIS ISLAND
INDEPENDENCE HALL
THE JEFFERSON MEMORIAL
THE LIBERTY BELL
THE LINCOLN MEMORIAL
MOUNT RUSHMORE
THE NATIONAL ANTHEM
THE PLEDGE OF ALLEGIANCE
ROCK 'N' ROLL
THE STATUE OF LIBERTY
UNCLE SAM
VIETNAM VETERANS MEMORIAL
THE WASHINGTON MONUMENT
THE WHITE HOUSE

THE
DECLARATION
OF
INDEPENDENCE

HAL MARCOVITZ

MASON CREST PUBLISHERS
PHILADELPHIA

Copyright © 2003 by Mason Crest Publishers. All rights
reserved. Printed and bound in the Hashemite Kingdom
of Jordan.

First printing

1 3 5 7 9 8 6 4 2

Library of Congress Cataloging-in-Publication Data
on file at the Library of Congress

ISBN 1-59084-038-0

Publisher's note: all quotations in this book come
from original sources, and contain the spelling and
grammatical inconsistencies of the original text.

American Symbols
AND THEIR Meanings

CONTENTS

Introduction

THE IMPORTANCE OF AMERICAN SYMBOLS

Symbols are not merely ornaments to admire—they also tell us stories. If you look at one of them closely, you may want to find out why it was made and what it truly means. If you ask people who live in the society in which the symbol exists, you will learn some things. But by studying the people who created that symbol and the reasons why they made it, you will understand the deepest meanings of that symbol.

The United States owes its identity to great events in history, and the most remarkable American Symbols are rooted in these events. The struggle for independence from Great Britain gave America the Declaration of Independence, the Liberty Bell, the American flag, and other images of freedom. The War of 1812 gave the young country a song dedicated to the flag, "The Star-Spangled Banner," which became our national anthem. Nature gave the country its national animal, the bald eagle. These symbols established the identity of the new nation, and set it apart from the nations of the Old World.

To be emotionally moving, a symbol must strike people with a sense of power and unity. But it often takes a long time for a new symbol to be accepted by all the people, especially if there are older symbols that have gradually lost popularity. For example, the image of Uncle Sam has replaced Brother Jonathan, an earlier representation of the national will, while the Statue of Liberty has replaced Columbia, a woman who represented liberty to Americans in the early 19th century. Since then, Uncle Sam and the Statue of Liberty have endured and have become cherished icons of America.

Of all the symbols, the Statue of Liberty has perhaps the most curious story, for unlike other symbols, Americans did not create her. She was created by the French, who then gave her to America. Hence, she represented not what Americans thought of their country but rather what the French thought of America. It was many years before Americans decided to accept this French goddess of Liberty as a symbol for the United States and its special role among the nations: to spread freedom and enlighten the world.

This series of books is valuable because it presents the story of each of America's great symbols in a freshly written way and will contribute to the students' knowledge and awareness of them. It is to be hoped that this information will awaken an abiding interest in American history, as well as in the meanings of American symbols.

—Barry Moreno,
librarian and historian
Ellis Island/Statue of Liberty National Monument

When British soldiers invaded Washington, D.C., in the summer of 1814, they found the city empty. Panicked citizens had fled when they heard the Redcoats were coming. Though the soldiers burned the White House and other important buildings, the nation's most important documents had been saved— including the Declaration of Independence.

FLIGHT TO LEESBURG

Just 29 years after America won its *independence* from Great Britain, the two nations were at war again. The British had never fully accepted their defeat at the hands of the *colonists* in the War for Independence. Meanwhile, the British continued *skirmishing* with the French, their long-time enemies, particularly on the high seas. Britain needed sailors for its navy, and in 1802, English warships started kidnapping American sailors and pressing them into service. Next, the British openly attacked American ships sailing for France. Finally, on June 18, 1812, America declared war on Britain. The War of 1812 had begun.

By August 1814, British troops had landed south of Washington and were marching toward the young nation's *capital*. John Armstrong, the secretary of war in the *cabinet* of *President* James Madison, had convinced himself that the British would not attack Washington. Other cabinet members disagreed with Armstrong. Meanwhile, citizens rushed to evacuate the city.

At the State Department, a senior clerk named Stephen Pleasanton had been ordered to save the young nation's most important *documents.* He found some heavy bags and started carrying out the orders. Along with treaties and other important documents, Pleasanton removed the *Declaration* of Independence— the original document signed by the *delegates* to the Continental *Congress* in Philadelphia 38 years before. The declaration outlined the *grievances* of the colonies toward the *king* of England, and announced that the

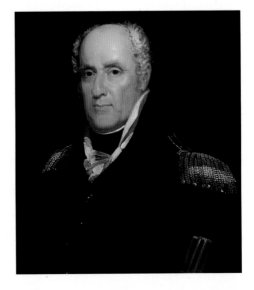

John Armstrong had been a general in the Continental Army during the American Revolution. In 1813 President James Madison appointed Armstrong secretary of war. Armstrong was so confident that the British would not attack the capital at Washington, D.C. that he did not set up a strong defense for the city. He and other leaders were forced to flee when British troops arrived in August 1814.

colonies would from then on be a new nation—the United States of America.

Pleasanton carefully rolled up the declaration and placed it in one of the *linen* bags. He found several carts and loaded them with the 22 linen bags of documents from the State Department. The carts were towed by mules across the Potomac River, then taken two miles upstream to the village of Georgetown, where they were hidden in an abandoned *gristmill*.

After a night in the gristmill, Pleasanton had the carts loaded again and driven to the town of Leesburg, Virginia, some 35 miles west of Washington. The bags were placed in an empty house. Pleasanton turned the keys over to John Littlejohn, a minister and the local sheriff of Leesburg.

When the British soldiers arrived in Washington, they found the city nearly empty. The soldiers set fire to the White House. Although a thunderstorm drenched the fire, extinguishing the flames before the building was completely destroyed, all that remained were the sturdy exterior walls of the mansion.

But far away in Leesburg, the papers saved by Stephen Pleasanton were safe from the British invasion. The papers were returned to Washington that fall. For saving the Declaration of Independence, Pleasanton received a promotion.

As for John Armstrong, his refusal to believe the British would invade Washington cost him his job.

British troops fire on the minutemen at Lexington, Massachusetts, in April 1775. Though the Redcoats routed the colonial militia in their first encounter, the minutemen would soon fight back, harassing the British until they returned to their base in Boston. The shots fired at Lexington and Concord were the first of the American Revolution.

JACOB GRAFF'S BOARDER

*T*homas Jefferson arrived in Philadelphia on June 11, 1776. He found the nation's largest city alive with talk of *revolution*. Since April of the previous year, when Massachusetts minutemen chased British soldiers out of the towns of Lexington and Concord, the colonies had been at war with the army of King George III.

The early months of the war had gone well for the colonists. They scored victories at Bunker Hill and Ticonderoga. Now, the Continental Army under George Washington was camped near New York, awaiting the arrival of a British invasion force. Ninety miles south of Washington's camp, delegates from the 13 colonies gathered in Philadelphia to put the official sanction of their governments on the Revolution. They would be meeting as members of the Continental Congress.

Jefferson was a delegate from Virginia. He was a wealthy *plantation* owner as well as a man of many talents. He practiced law, studied *architecture,* and was a dedicated reader and collector of books.

Among the delegates, there was agreement that they would have to take bold action. In May, the Continental Congress learned that King George had signed a treaty with the government of Germany, which agreed to provide him with 12,000 Hessian soldiers, troops who came from the German province of Hesse. This last act of King George—to hire *mercenaries* to destroy the Continental Army—erased any doubt the delegates may have had about the justness of the Revolution. Now, the delegates felt little loyalty to the king.

On May 15, the *legislature* of the Colony of Virginia instructed its delegates to the Congress to "propose to that respectable body to declare the United Colonies free and independent states."

On June 7, Virginia delegate Richard Henry Lee made that motion in the congress. Delegates decided to take up the question of independence in July. To prepare for their historic debate, members of the Congress appointed Jefferson and delegates Benjamin Franklin, John Adams, Roger Sherman, and Robert R. Livingston to a "committee to prepare a declaration to the effect of the said resolution." The job of what became known as the Committee of Five would be to set down in writing the reasons Congress would need to declare America's independence from England.

In Philadelphia, Jefferson took a room on the second

Thomas Jefferson was 33 years old when he joined the Committee of Five and was assigned the task of writing the Declaration of Independence. He was a lawyer, scholar, and owner of a 5,000-acre plantation in Virginia. Jefferson also had an interest in architecture: he designed his home in Virginia, which he named "Monticello" (Italian for "Little Mountain") and later submitted a design for the White House in Washington.

During the War for Independence, Jefferson served a term as governor of Virginia. After the war he was a minister to France. In 1789, George Washington appointed him secretary of state. He was elected to a term as vice president in 1796, then was elected president in 1800.

Under President Jefferson, the nation expanded its borders through the Louisiana Purchase. Thirteen future states would be formed out of the western territory that Jefferson obtained from France for about $15 million. He assigned the explorers William Clark and Meriwether Lewis the job of blazing a trail through the new territory. After a two-year mission Lewis and Clark returned with maps and descriptions of the vast land. Soon the territory would be opened to settlement by thousands of American pioneers.

floor of a three-story boarding house at Market and Seventh streets owned by Jacob Graff, a bricklayer.

Franklin, Adams, and the other members of the Committee of Five asked Jefferson to write the declaration. Jefferson worked on the document for 17 days, laboring over the words in his room while the delegates to the Continental Congress gathered to talk about independence in Philadelphia's State House just a few blocks away.

Born in 1735, John Adams of Massachusetts was a key figure in America's fight for independence. He was named to the Committee of Five by the other delegates to the Continental Congress, and given responsibility for framing the Declaration of Independence.

He turned that job over to Thomas Jefferson, a delegate from Virginia. Although the words in the final draft of the declaration are for the most part Jefferson's, Adams was the declaration's most vocal supporter during the debate on independence in late June and early July of 1776.

During the War for Independence, Adams served as a diplomat in Europe, recruiting allies for the colonies. He also helped negotiate the peace treaty with England that ended the war in 1783.

Following the war, Adams became the first vice president of the new republic, elected alongside President George Washington. Adams served one term as president, then lost to Thomas Jefferson in the election of 1800.

Jefferson intended to draw his ideas from many sources. Certainly, his words would reflect the feelings of the colonists— there was no question they felt the king's rule was unfair. But also, Jefferson had read the words of many

> **Jacob Graff charged Thomas Jefferson 35 shillings a week for the use of a room on the second floor of his boarding house in Philadelphia. For 17 days, Jefferson worked on the Declaration of Independence in that room.**

philosophers and was influenced by their ideas about the rights of free people. Most influential, perhaps, was the Englishman John Locke, who lived from 1632 to 1704. Locke wrote that a nation's power should rest in the hands of its people, and that a government had the responsibility to protect people's rights and property. Locke also believed people had a duty to rise up in revolution against an unjust ruler.

Jefferson also drew inspiration for the declaration from fellow Virginian George Mason, who had written the "Declaration of Rights" for his colony's legislature. Mason's declaration was a set of laws Virginia adopted to protect the rights and property of its citizens. Mason's work would later serve as an inspiration to the framers of the U.S. *Constitution,* who included many of his ideas in the first 10 amendments to the Constitution, known as the Bill of Rights.

In the opening sentence of the declaration, Jefferson set the tone for the entire document:

> When in the Course of human events, it becomes necessary for one people to dissolve the political bands which have connected them with another, and to assume among the Powers of the earth, the separate and equal station to which the Laws of Nature and of Nature's God entitle them, a decent respect to the opinions of mankind requires that they should declare the causes which impel them to the separation.

Next, Jefferson spelled out what would become the declaration's most important message to the king:

> We hold these truths to be self-evident, that all men are created equal, that they are endowed by their Creator with certain unalienable Rights, that among these are Life, Liberty and the pursuit of Happiness.

Jefferson had established that all men and women had the same rights, regardless of whether they were born rich or poor, and those rights included the right to live free. He said those rights were granted by God—the Creator—and that they were "self-evident," meaning men and women should expect to enjoy those rights whether the government said so or not.

His next words were aimed directly at King George. He said that when people disagree with their government, they have the right to "alter or to abolish it, and to institute new Government."

In England and many

Thomas Jefferson wrote the Declaration of Independence on a portable desk that he had designed himself.

Benjamin Franklin was 70 years old when, as a member of the Continental Congress, he voted for the Declaration of Independence.

Born in Boston in 1706, Franklin worked in his brother James's printing business, but in 1723 the brothers had a falling out and Benjamin left for Philadelphia. By 1729 he was the owner of the *Pennsylvania Gazette*, and soon transformed it into an influential newspaper in what was becoming America's largest city.

Meanwhile, he became active in Pennsylvania government. His name appears in the minutes of the first meeting of the Pennsylvania Provincial Assembly held in the State House on October 14, 1736, when he was appointed clerk of the assembly. In 1750, he won election to the assembly. From that point on Franklin was a major influence on the politics and government of both Pennsylvania and America.

After the declaration was adopted and signed, Franklin served as a diplomat in France. He returned to Philadelphia in 1785, where two years later he helped to draft the United States Constitution. He died in 1790 at the age of 84. One of his last pursuits was establishment of the Philadelphia Abolition Society, which urged the government to outlaw slavery.

other countries of the world, rulers held their thrones under what was known as "divine right," meaning they believed God had picked them and their families to rule.

But Jefferson's declaration said that would not be the case in America—the people would pick their leaders, and if the citizens disagreed with the way those leaders governed the nation, the people would have the right to pick new leaders.

Now, Jefferson got down to the specific grievances the colonists had against the king.

> He has refused his Assent to Laws, the most wholesome and necessary for the public good. . . . He has dissolved Representative Houses. . . . He has obstructed the Administration of Justice, by refusing his Assent to Laws for establishing Judiciary Powers. . . . He has kept among us, in times of peace, Standing Armies without the Consent of our legislature. . . . He has plundered our seas, ravaged our Coasts, burnt our towns, and destroyed the lives of our people.

Those words listed some of the complaints. In the final draft Jefferson listed many more. Essentially, all the complaints placed in the declaration by Jefferson came down to the belief by the colonists that the king would not let them rule themselves. Jefferson wrote:

> A Prince, whose character is thus marked by every act which may define a Tyrant, is unfit to be the ruler of a free People.

Finally, Jefferson ended by stating the intentions of the Continental Congress to separate the 13 colonies from the rule of the king—to declare independence.

> We, therefore, the Representatives of the united States of America, in General Congress, Assembled, appealing to the

Supreme Judge of the world for the rectitude of our intentions, do, in the Name, and by Authority of the good People
of these Colonies, solemnly publish and declare, That these
United Colonies are, and of Right ought to be Free and
Independent States; that they are Absolved from all
Allegiance to the British Crown, and that all political
connection between them and the State of Great Britain, is
and ought to be totally dissolved; and that as Free and
Independent States, they have full Power to levy War,
conclude Peace, contract Alliances, establish Commerce,
and to do all other Acts and Things which Independent
States may of right do. And for the support of this
Declaration, with a firm reliance on the protection of Divine
Providence, we mutually pledge to each other our Lives,
our Fortunes and our sacred Honor.

Jefferson completed the Declaration of Independence
on June 28. He showed it to Adams, Franklin, and the
other members of the Committee of Five. They made a
few changes, but for the most part the words that
Thomas Jefferson had written on the second floor of
Jacob Graff's rooming house would be the words
debated in just a few days by the delegates to the
Continental Congress.

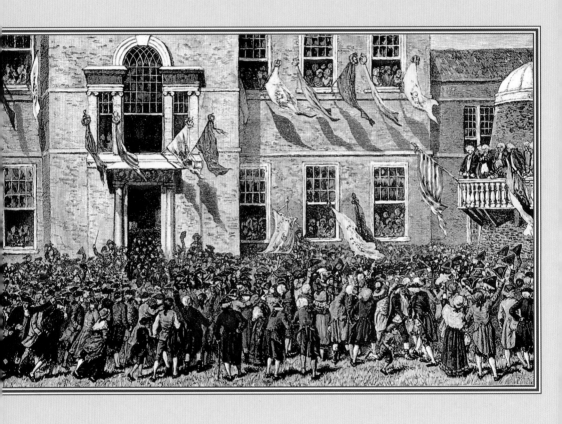

John Nixon, a colonel in the Continental Army, reads the Declaration of Independence in Philadelphia on July 8, 1776. "The greatest question was decided which ever was debated in America, and a greater perhaps, never was or will be decided among men," John Adams later wrote. "It is the will of heaven that the two countries should be sundered forever."

A BOLD ACT OF DEFIANCE

*J*ust before 9 A.M. on July 4, 1776, the 56 delegates to the Continental Congress started filing into the State House in Philadelphia. The building had been erected 40 years before as the home of the Pennsylvania *Assembly*. Now, members of the assembly agreed to conduct their business elsewhere, making the red-brick building available to the Congress.

Two days earlier, Congress had voted in favor of the June 7 resolution offered by Richard Henry Lee, which stated: "That these United Colonies are, and of right ought to be, free and independent States, that they are absolved from all allegiance to the British Crown, and that all political connection between them and the State of Great Britain is, and ought to be, totally dissolved."

Now, on July 4, the Congress intended to vote specifically on the declaration drafted by Jefferson. "This morning is assigned to the greatest debate of all," wrote John Adams.

The delegates entered the Philadelphia State House through the large doorway facing Chestnut Street. Above the door hung the royal *coat of arms*—the final reminder to them that they were still living under the oppressive will of the King of England.

The delegates met in the white-paneled meeting room on the east side of the building. Above, an elaborate crystal chandelier provided candle light. There were two fireplaces in the room and tall windows lining the walls. Displayed in the room were a British drum, swords, and flag captured in 1775 by Continental Army soldiers under the command of Ethan Allen at the battle of Fort Ticonderoga.

At the front of the room stood the president's *dais*— a raised table and chair usually occupied by the speaker of the Pennsylvania Assembly. On July 4, 1776, delegate John Hancock of Massachusetts sat at that table, having been named president of the Congress by the other delegates.

Hancock dropped the gavel to open the debate. One by one, delegates from the 13 colonies took turns making their arguments on independence.

In the final few days leading up to July 4, there had not been *unanimous* support for the declaration. Franklin urged the delegates opposing independence to change their minds. He said the vote had to be unanimous or the struggle would surely fail. He warned the delegates that if the war was lost, King George would send them to the *gallows*. He said: "We must all hang together, or assuredly we will all hang separately."

The declaration was read. Changes were made; most of the changes were minor, but there was one significant alteration—a passage blaming King George for the slave trade was removed from the final draft.

Finally, a roll call vote was taken. One by one, the delegates stood at their desks in the State House and voted in favor of independence. All delegates but those representing New York cast their ballots for independence. The New York delegates did not vote. They were waiting for instructions from the New York Assembly, which was still debating the issue of independence. On July 9, the New York Assembly cast its ballot for independence, making the vote unanimous.

At first, the declaration received just two signatures—those of Hancock, the president of the Congress, and Charles Thomson, the secretary. Later, the signatures of the other delegates were added.

Hancock signed his name in grand style, using a large and elaborate signature that clearly dominates the *parchment* below the words of the declaration and stands out from the other signatures. It was a bold act of defiance by the president of the Congress, showing the British that he had no regrets about putting his name to the words condemning the rule of the king.

Following its adoption, the declaration was sent to a

John Hancock of Boston, Massachusetts, was born the son of a humble preacher who died when the boy was just 7 years old. By the time he signed the Declaration of Independence 32 years later, Hancock was one of the wealthiest men in America. He owed his wealth largely to his Uncle Thomas, who adopted him following the death of his father. His uncle was a trader in tea, codfish, and whale oil. When Thomas Hancock died, his 27-year-old nephew John inherited his estate.

John Hancock believed in independence. In the years leading up to the American Revolution he supported rebellion and used his personal wealth to help the cause. In 1770, when five members of a Boston mob were killed by British troops in what became known as the Boston Massacre, Hancock spoke out publicly against Britain's military leaders.

He was elected president of the Continental Congress in 1776. This was mostly a ceremonial post; the job had little impact on the writing of the declaration. Nevertheless, he made his mark in history by making his mark—his large and elaborate signature on the declaration is easily one of America's most recognizable symbols. Legend has it that he wrote his name large enough "so the king wouldn't miss it."

printer to produce copies. Copies were distributed to a number of people the next day and sent to General Washington in the field. However, most Americans were still unaware that their government had announced their independence from England.

At 11 o'clock on the morning of July 8, the great bell—which would come to be known as the Liberty Bell—in the State House steeple started to *peal*, calling citizens of Philadelphia to the public square for what was sure to be an important announcement.

The people of Philadelphia had known the declaration was forthcoming. Hundreds of citizens flocked to the public square.

Just past noon, Colonel John Nixon, an officer in the Continental Army, strode out of the State House, scaled the steps of a platform in the courtyard, and read the Declaration of Independence to the American people. When Colonel Nixon finished, the bell in the State House steeple started ringing. In the crowd, people shouted: "God bless the free states of North America!"

And then nine soldiers from Pennsylvania marched to the Chestnut Street entrance of the State House and, as hundreds of Americans cheered, ceremoniously removed the royal coat of arms from above the door. Later that night, the coat of arms was burned in a huge bonfire lit by the new citizens of America to celebrate their freedom.

A Declaration by the Representatives of the UNITED STATES OF AMERICA, in General Congress assembled.

When in the course of human events it becomes necessary for one people to dissolve the political bands which have connected them with another, and to ~~assume~~ as-sume among the powers of the earth the separate and equal station to which the laws of nature & of nature's god entitle them, a decent respect to the opinions of mankind requires that they should declare the causes which impel them to the separation.

We hold these truths to be self-evident, that all men are created equal, that they are endowed by their creator with ~~inherent &~~ inalienable rights; that among these are life, & liberty, & the pursuit of happiness; that to secure these rights, go-vernments are instituted among men, deriving their just powers from the consent of the governed: that whenever any form of government becomes destructive of these ends, it is the right of the people to alter or to abolish it, & to institute new government, laying it's foundation on such principles, & organising it's powers in such form, as to them shall seem most likely to effect their safety & happiness. prudence indeed will dictate that governments long established should not be changed for light & transient causes: and accordingly all experience hath shewn that mankind are more disposed to suffer while evils are sufferable, than to right themselves by abolishing the forms to which they are accustomed. but when a long train of abuses & usurpations [begun at a distinguished period, &] pursuing invariably the same object, evinces a design to reduce them under absolute Despotism, it is their right, it is their duty, to throw off such government & to provide new guards for their future security. such has been the patient sufferance of these colonies; & such is now the necessity which constrains them to alter their former systems of government. the history of the present king of Great Britain is a history of unremitting injuries and usurpations, [among which, appears no solitary fact to contra--dict the uniform tenor of the rest [all of which have] in direct object the establishment of an absolute tyranny over these states. to prove this, let facts be submitted to a candid world, [for the truth of which we pledge a faith yet unsullied by falsehood.]

A draft of the Declaration of Independence, in Thomas Jefferson's handwriting. In the summer of 1776 the Continental Congress created a five-member committee to write the declaration; however, Jefferson was the main author of the document.

THE WORDS OF THOMAS JEFFERSON

The Netherlands is a tiny storybook country in Europe; a place where windmills still grind corn, tulips blossom in the fields, and dairies produce some of the world's best-loved cheeses.

But the country, which is also known as Holland, suffered through a bloody past. In the 1500s, Holland was under the rule of a Spanish prince who had little love for the Dutch people or their land. To the Dutch people, Prince Philip was a tyrant and they ached for freedom.

In 1568, they rose up against Philip's rule. Led by Prince William of Orange, the Dutch fought against the Spanish army. With the help of the powerful British

Thomas Jefferson and John Adams both died on July 4, 1826—the 50th anniversary of the adoption of the Declaration of Independence.

navy, they succeeded in driving the Spaniards out of Holland in 1588.

The rebellion by the Dutch against Prince Philip is notable because in 1581 leaders of the revolution wrote their own declaration of independence. The Dutch declaration is believed to be the first time in history that an oppressed people set down in writing their rights and grievances as well as their intentions to break away from a tyrant. The Dutch declaration bears some similarity to the document written by Jefferson.

For example, Jefferson said, "A Prince, whose character is thus marked by every act which may define a Tyrant, is unfit to be the ruler of a free people."

He was, of course, talking about King George, but the Dutch had similar words about Prince Philip. Their declaration said:

> A prince is constituted by God to be ruler of a people, to defend them from oppression and violence as the shepherd his sheep. . . . And when he does not behave thus, but, on the contrary, oppresses them, seeking opportunities to infringe their ancient customs and privileges, exacting from them slavish compliance, then he is no longer a prince, but a tyrant, and the subjects are to consider him in no other view.

The major difference between the American and

Two armies collide during the Dutch War for Independence in the late 16th century. The Dutch wrote their own declaration of independence nearly 200 years before the American Revolution.

Dutch declarations, though, is that the American declaration was written by common people who wished to kick out a king and govern themselves. The Dutch declaration was written by men who wished to kick out a bad king from another country so they could be ruled by a king of their own choosing.

When the Americans won their independence from King George, the idea that people could govern themselves spread throughout Europe. Soon, revolution erupted in France. In 1789, an assembly of French citizens adopted the "Declaration of the Rights of Man and

The people of France helped the American colonists gain their freedom from Great Britain during the revolution. In 1789, six years after the American Revolution ended, the French rose up against their own king. This painting shows one of the most famous moments of the French Revolution, the storming of a royal prison called the Bastille by a mob of French citizens. The French Revolution had been intended to create a democratic government like that of the United States; in fact, the French Declaration of the Rights of Man and of the Citizen was modeled on the Declaration of Independence. However, the revolution failed to create a stable, permanent democracy. By 1799 the French Republic had fallen and Napoleon Bonaparte ruled the country .

of the Citizen." There is no question the words in the French declaration were inspired by the words written by Jefferson just 13 years before.

The French declaration said: "Men are born and remain free and equal in rights. Social distinctions may be found only upon the general good. The aim of all political association is the preservation of the natural rights of man. These rights are liberty, property, security and resistance to oppression."

In the years since then, other countries have written similar documents to declare their independence. In 1848, the people of Hungary issued their own Declaration of Independence. At the time, the Hungarians were ruled by Austrian Emperor Franz Joseph I. Alas, Franz Joseph crushed the Hungarian rebellion. Hungary would not win its freedom from Austria until World War I, when the armies of America and the democracies of Europe defeated Austria and Germany on the battle-field.

For centuries, the people of Japan had been ruled by emperors and dictators. Following World War II, when the Japanese were defeated by the armies of

> **Philadelphia printer John Dunlap made copies of the declaration on the night of July 4, 1776. At least 25 of those copies are known to exist today. One of them was found in a cheap glass frame at a flea market and later sold at auction for $8.4 million.**

America and the other free nations, the people of Japan wanted to write their own constitution—a set of laws to govern themselves.

In 1946, the authors of Japan's constitution drew their

> In 1940, during an attempt to repair the case that held the declaration, Library of Congress employees inadvertently splattered glue on the document.

inspiration from the words of Thomas Jefferson. Indeed, the Japanese constitution states that the "fundamental human rights guaranteed to the people by this Constitution . . . include the right to life, liberty, and the pursuit of happiness."

Declarations of independence aren't always issued with the best of intentions. In Africa, the nation of Zimbabwe had been ruled for nearly a century by Great Britain. At the time, the nation was known as Rhodesia. In the early 1960s, Rhodesians started fighting for independence. The British opposed independence for the African nation, but chose not to employ force to keep the country under the British flag. On November 11, 1965, Rhodesian Prime Minister Ian D. Smith issued a declaration of independence.

Once again, the author of a declaration of independence found inspiration in the words of Thomas Jefferson. In 1776, Jefferson started the American declaration with the words, "When in the Course of human events." Those words gave a historical significance to the declaration that followed.

Ian Smith regarded Rhodesia's independence on the same historical plane. "We are a determined people who have been called upon to play a role of world-wide significance," he wrote.

History would prove him correct, but not for the reasons he imagined. Britain had opposed Rhodesia's independence because Smith wanted to establish a government ruled by white citizens only. By 1978, leaders of the black majority planned an overthrow of the white government. With the likelihood of an armed rebellion approaching, the whites of Rhodesia gave in to the black majority, which took control of the government and changed the name of the country to Zimbabwe.

African slaves are unloaded at the English colony in Jamestown, Virginia, in 1619. Though in 1776 the Declaration of Independence stated that all men are equal, slavery continued in the United States until 1865. In fact, many of the Founding Fathers, including Thomas Jefferson, who wrote the Declaration of Independence, were slaveholders.

"ALL MEN ARE CREATED EQUAL"

African slaves first arrived on American shores in 1619, when a Dutch ship sailed into the harbor of Jamestown, Virginia, and sold 20 slaves to the colonists. They were soon put to work in the nearby tobacco fields. More than a century and a half later, when Thomas Jefferson sat down in his rented room in Philadelphia to draft the Declaration of Independence, thousands of slaves were owned by plantation owners throughout the South. The planters relied on slaves for cheap labor. In fact, Jefferson himself owned slaves.

And yet, Jefferson as well as other colonial leaders had started questioning slavery. Thomas Paine, whose stirring words demanding freedom from British *tyranny* would inspire Washington's men at the Battle of Trenton, said a "slave, who is proper owner of his freedom, has the right to reclaim it, however often sold."

Benjamin Franklin was another opponent of slavery. Following the War for Independence, Franklin was a founder of the Pennsylvania *Abolition* Society. On February 12, 1790—just a few weeks before his death—Franklin signed a petition submitted to Congress, calling for the federal government to outlaw slavery.

By the time the Continental Congress met in Philadelphia, most of the nations of the world had outlawed slavery. Even England ended slavery in 1772.

Jefferson made a statement against slavery in the declaration. He accused King George of permitting slaves to be introduced into the colonies. He called slavery "a cruel war against human nature itself and violating its most sacred rights of life and liberty." The delegates from the southern colonies of South Carolina and Georgia objected. Fearing those delegates would walk out of the convention, and that the vote for independence would not be unanimous, Jefferson agreed to take the words regarding

The bell that summoned Philadelphians to the public square in front of the State House on July 8, 1776, to hear the first reading of the declaration was eventually adopted by people who opposed slavery. An Abolitionist pamphlet published in 1839 first referred to the bell as the "Liberty Bell."

The crowd at the battlefield at Gettysburg, where President Abraham Lincoln delivered his famous address. Lincoln was in Gettysburg on November 19, 1863, for the dedication of a cemetery for the soldiers who had fallen at Gettysburg. He can be seen in this photo; he is bareheaded and facing the camera, to the left of the central figure in the top hat.

slavery out of the declaration.

Following the War for Independence, black slaves remained in bondage in America. By the outbreak of the Civil War in 1861, 4 million slaves would be performing forced labor on plantations in the Southern states.

In the years that followed, the abolitionist movement

A handwritten copy of Lincoln's Gettysburg Address, on paper with the White House's letterhead. Delivered 87 years after the Declaration of Independence was written, the Gettysburg Address asserted again that in America, all men are created equal, whether black or white. After the Civil War, the Thirteenth Amendment was added to the U.S. Constitution; it forever ended slavery in the United States.

slowly gained fervor, with Northerners calling for the end of slavery and Southerners demanding "states' rights," meaning they wished to determine for themselves whether to keep slavery. Finally, the furor over the issue erupted into the Civil War.

On November 19, 1863, President Abraham Lincoln traveled to Gettysburg, Pennsylvania. Just a few months earlier, the Union Army had won a decisive yet bloody victory there against the army of the Confederacy. The battle of Gettysburg had turned the tide of the war in favor of the Union Army, and would mark the beginning of the final chapter in the Civil War, and along with it the end of slavery in America.

Lincoln arrived in Gettysburg to help dedicate a national cemetery established on the battlefield. The president was not expected to be the major speaker of the day so he only made a short speech. In fact, he spoke for less than three minutes.

But in the Gettysburg Address, Lincoln told the audience that the signers of the Declaration of Independence meant all men—whether they are white or black—are created equal, and that all Americans deserve the rights and freedoms that were put down in words on parchment by Thomas Jefferson just 87 years before the battle of Gettysburg.

He said: "Four score and seven years ago, our fathers brought forth upon this continent a new nation: conceived in liberty, and dedicated to the proposition that all men are created equal."

1776 Thomas Jefferson arrives in Philadelphia on June 11 and begins working on the Declaration of Independence in Jacob Graff's boarding house; on July 2, delegates to the Continental Congress approve a resolution calling for independence from England; on July 4, the Declaration of Independence is adopted by the Continental Congress; on July 8, the declaration read for the first time in public.

1814 Clerk Stephen Pleasanton rescues the declaration from British troops by hiding it in Leesburg, Virginia.

1823 Newspapers report the ink on the declaration is fading.

1841 The declaration is displayed on the wall of the U.S. Patent Office, where it will suffer damage from sunlight for 35 years.

1863 On November 19, President Abraham Lincoln delivers the Gettysburg Address, insisting the declaration's promise that "all men are created equal" applies to slaves as well.

1876 The declaration is displayed in Philadelphia during the Centennial National Exposition.

1883 The declaration is enclosed in a steel vault that is light-proof and air-tight.

1924 A new vault is erected for the declaration and U.S. Constitution at the Library of Congress.

1941 The Declaration of Independence and U.S. Constitution are stored at Fort Knox in Kentucky until the end of World War II.

1951 A new vault is erected for the declaration and constitution at the National Archives building.

abolition—the act of ending slavery. Prior to the Civil War, a person who called for an end to slavery was called an abolitionist.

architecture—the character and design of buildings and other public structures.

assembly—the governing body of a state, composed of representatives elected by the people. This is sometimes referred to as the legislature.

cabinet—the top advisers to a president; in America, cabinet members head federal departments.

capital—a city that serves as the official center of government for a state or nation.

coat of arms—the elaborate symbol of a family.

colonists—a group of people who settle in a new land and form a community.

Congress—the lawmaking branch of the American government.

constitution—the document containing the laws of a state or nation.

dais—a raised platform, as in a hall or large room.

declaration—a formal and official announcement.

delegates—representatives to a meeting, often a political convention.

document—a paper containing written information, usually regarded as the official position of a person or organization.

gallows—a structure from which criminals are hanged.

grievances—complaints, often voiced in written form.

gristmill—a mill for grinding grain.

independence—freedom from the rule of others.

king—the leader of a nation whose right to rule is guaranteed by birth.

44 GLOSSARY

legislature—an organized body of persons having the authority to make laws for a political unit.

linen—coarse material woven from flax.

mercenary—a soldier hired for service in the army of a foreign country.

parchment—the skin of sheep or goats used for a writing material.

peal—the sound made by bells.

philosopher—a person who offers his views to questions that may not have clear-cut answers.

plantation—a large farm that grows cotton, tobacco, coffee and similar crops.

president—the chief executive of a government whose authority is provided by a vote of the people.

revolution—the forcible overthrow of a government.

skirmish—a minor dispute or contest between opposing parties.

tyranny—the harsh rule of a king.

unanimous—complete agreement by all parties on a particular issue.

FURTHER READING

Ferry, Joseph. *The Jefferson Memorial.* Philadelphia: Mason Crest Publishers, 2003.

Marcovitz, Hal. *Independence Hall.* Philadelphia: Mason Crest Publishers, 2003.

Miller, Douglas T. *Thomas Jefferson and the Creation of America.* New York: Facts on File Inc., 1997.

Phelan, Mary Kay. *Four Days in Philadelphia.* New York: Thomas Y. Crowell Company, 1967.

Pitch, Anthony S. *The Burning of Washington.* Annapolis, Maryland: Naval Institute Press, 1998.

Severance, John B. *Thomas Jefferson: Architect of Democracy.* New York: Clarion Books, 1998.

Wagner, Frederick. *Patriot's Choice: The Story of John Hancock.* New York: Dodd, Mead and Company, 1964.

INTERNET RESOURCES

History of the Declaration of Independence

http://www.nara.gov/exhall/charters/declaration/dechist.html

http://memory.loc.gov/const/declar.html

http://www.loc.gov/exhibits/declara/declara1.html

http://www.yale.edu/lawweb/avalon/declare.htm

http://www.ushistory.org/declaration/

Declarations of independence in other countries

http://www.h-net.msu.edu/~habsweb/sourcetexts/hungind.html

http://chnm.gmu.edu/declaration/japanese/aruga2.html

http://www.fordham.edu/halsall/mod/1581dutch.html

http://www.fordham.edu/halsall/mod/1965Rhodesia-UDI.html

PICTURE CREDITS

BARRY MORENO has been librarian and historian at the Ellis Island Immigration Museum and the Statue of Liberty National Monument since 1988. He is the author of *The Statue of Liberty Encyclopedia*, which was published by Simon and Schuster in October 2000. He is a native of Los Angeles, California. After graduation from California State University at Los Angeles, where he earned a degree in history, he joined the National Park Service as a seasonal park ranger at the Statue of Liberty; he eventually became the monument's librarian. In his spare time, Barry enjoys reading, writing, and studying foreign languages and grammar. His biography has been included in *Who's Who Among Hispanic Americans*, *The Directory of National Park Service Historians*, *Who's Who in America*, and *The Directory of American Scholars*.

HAL MARCOVITZ is a journalist for *The Morning Call*, a newspaper based in Allentown, Pennsylvania. He has written more than 20 books for young readers. He lives in Chalfont, Pennsylvania, with his wife, Gail, and their daughters, Ashley and Michelle.